The Snare of
Assumptions

*The Deadly Effects of Assuming and
How God Heals Our Souls.*

Jennifer Kegin

authorHOUSE®

AuthorHouse™
1663 Liberty Drive
Bloomington, IN 47403
www.authorhouse.com
Phone: 1 (800) 839-8640

Published by AuthorHouse 03/09/2015

ISBN: 978-1-4969-7379-5 (sc)
ISBN: 978-1-4969-7378-8 (e)

Print information available on the last page.

Dedication

I dedicate this book to the many Believers who've struggled with assumptions and the deadly effects of assuming. May this book help them realize they are not alone and that God wants them set free of this bondage. And help the Believer (the Church) to recognize its place of authority over this battle.

Acknowledgements

I give all credit to my Savior and my King Jesus. I am grateful for the Holy Spirit's guidance to write this book. I also want to give a huge thank you to my husband, Kevin, for putting up with me in my ups and downs during this process. Also, thank you to my three daughters, Kristy, Lana and Amie for being my cheerleaders. Through everything, my family has been there. And a special thank you to Kelly Cook for my cover design. Thank You.

Contents

Introduction

"Our Purpose"

To begin this book I want to start with setting groundwork on God's purpose for His children. We should have only one purpose in life... To do the Father's will. But we must "know" His will to be able to DO His will. The way we "know" His will, is to read His Word. The Word edifies, judges, cleanses, corrects, guides and directs us.

I think so many of us choose not to read His Word because then we have to look at the real person inside of us. Most of the time, sad enough, we don't like ourselves. But the Word doesn't condemn us (as man does), it convicts and changes us. But The Process of Change is one of the hardest things to go through. It goes against the very nature of our flesh. Because our flesh wants to stay just as it is. But the Word will cleanse and make us white as snow.

Isaiah 1:18 "Come now, and let us reason together says the Lord; though your sins are like scarlet, they shall be white as snow."

As Believers, we tend to "bring up" our sin again and again... when our Father forgives our sin, and with His forgiveness, we can have a brand new slate. Our flesh can't wrap it's brain around true forgiveness. Therefore, we struggle and fight against the very One who loves us without condemnation.

When we do look into God's Word, we can receive His forgiveness, but we must realize we have to be cleansed to live out His holiness. His very heart is to love us unconditionally. We get lost in our flesh and condemn ourselves, while He is ready to receive us, regardless of where our minds have gone - where our mouth has spoken harsh words. He forgives, but we ponder and ponder until there is a "sore" in our brain... festering and poisonous.

This book was written during a very hard trial in my life. I was having thoughts of suicide and the Lord rescued me out of this state of depression. It was in this trial that I birthed this book. Having never written a book before, I was astonished that God used this time and hard trial to birth a book about assumptions.

And, I am fully convinced that the Holy Spirit used this trial to bring about this book. I am praying that as you read this book you get freedom from any bondages that have bound you or kept you from your God-given destiny. I am also in deep intercession for those who have gone through depression and thoughts of suicide. But, as you read this book I pray you find answers to questions you have asked of God. May God give you just the revelation that you need!! As I know He certainly did me!!

Chapter 1

"Assuming the Worst"

The very brain God made, that He created, goes to places of crazy thoughts and emotions that are not tamed. We "think" we know what others are thinking... when it's just a ploy of our enemy to keep us in a place of emotional assumptions. This, then, leads to our brain running through "what ifs". What if he doesn't care about me anymore? What if my mom and dad don't really love me?

We assume we know, when in all reality, our fleshly minds ran to areas of untruth, areas we have a hard time taming.

"Taming our minds." NOW that is a million dollar statement!!

> James 3:8 says "But no man can tame the tongue. It is
> an unruly evil, full of deadly poison."

But, if our minds are subject to our God, then our lips (our thoughts/ our tongue) will be subject also! I sit and shake my head, because you don't know how many zillioneth times my mind has taken me places too horrible to recall!! Then, of course, my lips follow suit.

But there is Good News! We CAN tame our minds with God's Word.

Hebrews 4:12 "For the word of God is living and powerful, and sharper than any two-edged sword, piercing even to the division of soul and spirit, and of joints and marrow, and is a discerner of the thoughts and intents of the heart."

But we must put our fleshly minds in subjection to God's Word and His will. If we are in subjection to Him… our minds are wrapped up in His love, His goodness. See the difference here? Fleshly assumptions… or godly thinking.

So, why do we even go there?? I mean, I've questioned my sanity at times because of all the awful thoughts running through my brain!!

Just for a minute, let's think back to Adam and Eve… what separated them from God? SIN. That dirty little 3-letter word! SIN. Separation from our Creator.

We don't want to talk about sin much anymore. Even our churches tend to "white wash" sin. But we all struggle with sin. It's just that God deals with our sin through Grace, Grace we can't quite comprehend. His Grace… without it, we are GONERS!! But with His Grace we have it made in the shade!! (heaven's shade!)

I would like to pray over everyone reading this right now. Please take a minute to reflect with God and listen to His voice…

Father God, I pray we get revelation about Your love and about Your forgiveness of sin, whether it's something we did today or a year ago. I pray Father that we know beyond any doubt that Your love covers all sin. And that You gave Your Son to die for each one of us and when He died on that cross, He bore everything for us!! Thank You, my Savior, for all You've done for us and for all You are going to do in the future. I am in awe how good You are to us, even when we don't obey You, You forgive us. Even when we don't follow You, You keep asking us to come back. Thank You for grace, mercy and love never-ending. Thank You for life eternal through Jesus' sacrifice. Amen

Notes and Reflections:

Notes and Reflections:

Chapter 2

"I Don't Have Pride!"

Before we get too far into this chapter, I want to talk about assumptions and what this word means. I looked in my dictionary to find the meaning, look how interesting this is...

Assumption = the act of taking for granted or supposing; presumption; arrogance

Then I was curious, arrogance... Here's what arrogance means...

Arrogance = overbearing pride!!

Pride? "But God, I don't have Pride, do I??" My next question to God was "Is my assuming coming from pride and arrogance?" The Holy Spirit answered my question... He told me "Pride makes you look at yourself above others." Ouch!

So, in my journey to find out what God said about Pride... Here are just a few in God's Word... Pride is in our hearts (Obadiah 1:3). Pride will make us fall (Proverbs 16:18). Pride is evil (Mark 7:22). And that is only a small selection of scriptures where God talks about Pride. There are more!!

Even as a small child I "assumed" people were talking about me... that people didn't like me... assuming without knowing.

Because assumptions come from our selfish desires, from our flesh, not from our spirit man... assumptions deceive and distort the very heart of God. We judge our brother and sister with assumptions. We judge the very people God has created in His image. Assumptions bring "unrighteous thinking" and bear our true self. How can I assume anything bad about God's very creation??

It's only in my pride... **only in my pride!!**

But, there is hope!! Hope for the fallen man. God is a merciful God, full of compassion for His people. Casting our sin as far as the East is to the West.

> *Psalm 103:12 "As far as the east is from the west, so far has He removed our transgressions from us."*

When we are learning who we are in Him - we must look into His Word. Our very Life Manual. Our map to our destiny lies in the marvelous pages of our Father's Word. This is where we glean... we soak in His truth. Where we begin to see His heart.

God's Word is intended to guide us in all we do. There are answers to all of lives questions in His Word. The easy questions and the hard questions.

My prayer for you is that you get a hunger to know God's Word like never before. That as you finish this book, you will not be satisfied until you search out His Word for yourself. It's in a relationship with God that you will begin to love His Word and start wanting to live His Word.

Soak in His Word and become saturated with His truth and love!! This is God's longing, to be closer to you than a brother.

Notes and Reflections:

Notes and Reflections:

Chapter 3

"Grace So Divine"

Grace: Pardon; Mercy; Unmerited favor and love of God

We want it, we long for it, for His Grace to really cover our sins - but - do we GET it?? I doubt it!! His Grace is beyond abundant and amazing. I wish right here I would get a new word just to describe His Grace!! But when we look at our sin compared to His Grace... it makes my heart smile and gives me a warmth only Grace can give. Like eternal life, that's forever!! There is nothing else in this life that's forever and eternally lasting.

> *Titus 3:7 "that having been justified by His grace we should become heirs according to the hope of eternal life."*

Grace has been here for us from the time we were still in our mother's womb.

> *Psalm 139:14 "For You formed my inward parts; You covered me in my mother's womb."*

Grace was around long before we could even count the years! And yet, we have trouble getting this down inside our "knower"!! Grace.

What if we started "assuming" with God's Word? I mean, WHAT IF?? It would sound like this... "Well, Grace is FOR me... then that means I'm forgiven of what I said!" Or... "Grace is really forever and ever, God really does want me to live with Him in heaven!!" See the stark difference here?? We begin to not only hear about Grace, but we begin to know His Grace. Really KNOW His Grace!!

Assumptions not only are "thoughts" but they become words. And as we well know, our very words can give life or death.

> *Proverbs 18:21 "Death and life are in the power of the*
> *tongue, and those who love it will eat its fruit."*

We have to recognize that while our lips are flesh... our minds can be renewed... Look at God's Word...

> *Romans 12:2 "And do not be conformed to this world,*
> *but be transformed by the renewing of your mind..."*

Our hearts, our souls can be transformed. It's not a "hit the easy button" sort of transformed. It takes reading His Word, sacrificing your time to meditate on His Word. Time with our Savior, letting His Presence engulf every aspect of our life. Yes, we can!! Read His Word... it's there for our benefit!!

As we are almost to the next chapter... Please, right here at this moment - just stop and talk to God. Ask Him for help. He will administer Grace over our lives. I am praying that as you read this you may recognize the Cross is your guarantee!!

The Cross, Grace… oh, the joy we sing! Christ, our Lord, the risen King!!

I get excited when I think what God did for us!! Beautiful picture of Grace, so divine. I mean, how could Someone love me that much?? Is it possible?? You look at the world today and there isn't much unconditional love going around. Even in our churches we've lost this Grace thing along the way. Somehow we've replaced His Grace with conforming to the world's view of Love.

Here again, please read His Word!! Find out for yourself about how awesome His Grace really is!! Don't settle for anything less than obtaining God's Grace. Once you figure out this Grace thing, you will be free from bondages of the past. Because once God's Grace becomes real to us… nothing in this life can steal it away.

My prayer for you, as we end this chapter on Grace together, is that you realize exactly who you are because of what He did.

Never "assume" anything without God's Word to back it up!! And always let His Grace cover your mistakes. Someday we have "perfect" to look forward to… until then… Let His Word lead you in all you do and in all you say!!

Notes and Reflections:

Notes and Reflections:

Chapter 4

"I've Changed My Mind"

The mind... The thoughts... The madness!

Our minds can be our greatest asset and our worst enemy. We must learn to control our emotions and our thoughts by striving to be as God created us to be.

We all deal with our fleshly mind, and I'm praying this book helps us to separate our fleshly mind and for us to recognize the mind of Christ. The Word tells us that if we believe in Christ, then we can have His mind!!

> *1 Corinthians 2:16 "For "who has known the mind of the Lord that he may instruct Him?" But we have the mind of Christ."*

But, remember, the enemy will "play" with our mind and our thoughts. He is out to kill, steal and to destroy us.

> *John 10:10 "The thief does not come except to steal, and to kill, and to destroy. I have come that they may have life, and that they may have it more abundantly."*

If we allow the enemy to control us in any form or fashion, he will take more than you bargain for.

During a difficult time in my life, I fought "thoughts" of suicide and I argued with my own mind. Hearing thoughts of.... "I don't feel worthy." And arguing... "I am a child of the Most High God!" I wrestled with an unseen (but very real) foe... the enemy of our souls. I had to take authority over my mind and my emotions.

Being a Christian, I knew that suicide was not the answer. Yet, at the time it seemed a way out, an escape from the fears of the unknown. An escape, a way of not facing myself, not facing the decisions I had made. But, all the while, I knew better. I knew that I had everything to live for and I also knew the enemy was having a hay day with my mind! But, it was a battle I've never faced before, only heard people talk about depression and about their attempts at suicide. Never dreaming I would someday have to fight the same dark battle.

When you've faced depression and suicide, you can really sympathize with others who have been there. I look at depression in a whole new light. And through it all, I have come to realize I am more than a conqueror!!

This is a scripture I quoted a lot during this rough season in my life...

Romans 8:37 "Yet in ALL these things we are more
than conquerors through Him who loved us."

I stood on the Word of God (my Life Line) and declared to the heavenlies and the principalities of the air that I would live and not die. I prayed violent prayers in my combat to win this battle.

Matthew 11: 12 "And from the days of John the Baptist
until now the kingdom of heaven suffers violence, and the
violent take it by force."

I am here to tell you, the battle is real. It's a battle of the very brain that sets above your neck!! The enemy will go to all lengths to take you out of the game of life.

In Christ, I've changed my mind!! How about you? If this is all too real to you... it seems I'm telling your story too... Please get real with yourself and tell someone how you're feeling and pray with them. Don't do this alone! It's a lie from our enemy to isolate us and make us feel like we are all alone. He will tell you lies...

John 8:44 "...because there is no truth in him (devil).
When he speaks a lie, he speaks from his own resources, for
he is a liar and the father of it."

Right at this moment... this time with me... this very minute... Face your enemy. He will certainly come after you with all he has. If you fight with God's Word, the Sword of the Spirit, you will win. But, if you sink in a corner and give up, the enemy has defeated another Child of God. Let's stand up and tell others how to fight and how to combat depression and suicidal issues.

I want to tell you of another struggle I've dealt with... There was a time in my adult life I didn't want to face anyone nor did I like myself. From thoughts and assumptions... I didn't want to hear anyone else's opinion of me, because I thought bad of myself. I "assumed" they felt the same way as I did. I would stay home alone, not going along with my husband... And during this time, I can remember him asking me "Don't you want to go with me?" I would tell him no, then when he was gone, I would wonder what was wrong with me. In assuming, I thought it better to just be alone. I isolated myself so much that it became a part of my life, not too normal though.

I was not fighting with God's awesome Word. Not realizing it, I had given up even before the fight began. But, Praise God, He has rescued me!! I am a new creation in Him. Every day His mercies are new toward us!!

Lamentations 3:23 "Great is His faithfulness; His mercies begin afresh each morning."

I have discovered His promises to stand on and I don't have to be alone. I don't have to face life's many trials without the saving Grace of my Father God. He was willing to send His Son to die for us, to guarantee our salvation. This is a promise we can stand on in every need.

So, have you "Changed Your Mind" to the very image of God?? If not, here's your chance.. Let's pray this prayer together...

Dear Father God, You are the God of second chances. I need a miracle in my life. I ask you in Jesus' mighty name to help me from this moment on to transform my mind into the image of Christ. I want to die to my flesh and be alive in You. Give me wisdom to discern whether or not the enemy is deceiving me. I want to walk worthy of Your call on my life. I do believe You have a plan for my life. Today, is a new day in You. I thank You for Your mercy, new every day!! I'm on my way to being a Word Believing Conqueror!! Amen

Notes and Reflections:

Notes and Reflections:

Chapter 5

"Weathering the Storm"

As I heard my grandson's video saying "Toby, the storm is really bad..." I thought about the storms of my Christian walk... the seasons of dark winds, that tried to overtake me. The seasons of harsh dry times of loneliness, and a despair that only comes from the enemy. The seasons of heartbreak and pain. The seasons we all will endure in this life. And how the enemy kept lying to me, making me assume that I'm the only one who suffers these storms.

Then I thought about the storm Jesus calmed... With just His words "Peace, be still."

> *Mark 4:39 "Then He arose and rebuked the wind, and said to the sea "Peace, be still!" And the wind ceased and there was a great calm."*

This passage gives me a new outlook on the storms that have invaded my life. If Jesus walked on the water, during this great storm, then why can't I walk on the water of life's storms too?? And since I have Him living inside me, then the storm doesn't look as bad. I mean from an angle of being over-the-storm, walking on top of the storm... This is the place where I would much rather be to weather these storms. Looking down upon the storm, with a life-saving trust in my Savior to carry me through.

The storms of life will surely come. So, I intend to be as ready as I possibly can to face them with tenacious faith. To face them with a determination that I'm not going to drown in the waves of hurt and disappointments.

Life can bring upon us hard trials of many kinds. But, Jesus promised us He would never leave us nor forsake us.

> *Deuteronomy 31:6 "Be strong and of good courage, do not fear nor be afraid of them; for the Lord our God, He is the One who goes with you. He will not leave you nor forsake you."*

If I can make it through just this season, keep my nose above the crashing waves... Then I can face the next storm of life. So, through every trial and every storm I weather, I lean on Him to see me through.

Have you ever noticed that a body of water can turn calm so quickly in a storm? Have you ever just sat and watched the waves on top of a body of water? My husband and I just went on a fishing trip. We both commented how calm it was on the water. How the wind had lain and it was so peaceful. As you picture this with me, isn't this a perfect picture of how God calms our storms and gives us a peace only He can give?

So, as you go through the storms of life, remember to walk above the waves, to trust in a Man who calms the seas.

Storms take on so many different forms in our life. Storms of losing a job, losing a loved one, sickness and disease, changes we didn't expect, and many more storms. But we must trust in God to see us through and to use every storm to become stronger in Him.

As a Believer, we must walk above the storms... to shine our light to a dark world, full of hopelessness. If we don't weather the storms of life, then the world has no hope. It's in our hope that the world begins to search for Him. It's through our "walking on the waves" that the world comes to believe in our Savior. It's in our faith that the world is able to look right into the face of God.

We must keep our noses above the water to survive the storms. As sobering as this seems, the storms will come and the storms will go. But it's in these troubled times that we grow and begin to walk on the waves of life, we begin to trust in Him. All the while the world is watching our progress. The world is looking at us. They are wondering what we will do during the storms of life.

Christian Believers, must walk above the waves and bring the drowning lost world onto the shore of life. How will you handle the storms of life? Because, someone IS watching you!!

Notes and Reflections:

Notes and Reflections:

Chapter 6

"Christian Believer, Get Up!"

My inspiration for this book came from a tough spot in my life. But my saving Grace came from the very pages of my Bible. God's Word encompasses our freedom. Freedom from the prideful art of fleshly assuming. Assuming we are right, when in all actuality, we are wrong. But God's Word cuts through the lies and deception of our enemy and sets us free with a clean cut of truth.

I picture His Word as the sword of truth cutting and pruning away my pride. Oh, how this hurts my flesh! How my mind fights back! But when all the pruning is ended, all the pride is stripped away... in this, God attaches Himself to me, cleansing me with His love. In the end, it's all worth it. Because now I see the truth. Pride exposed. His truth enters in like a Knight in shining armor. Saving me, from me. And yet, one more time I'm face to face with a perfect Savior. My sin vanishes, only to be found on the other side of Grace. Exposure to truth. Never to be the same. Changed by Grace.

There is a season of change coming upon Christian Believers... There is a cry from God Himself to live a holy life... to take the higher road of righteous living. If we are to bring in the harvest, we must first become truthful with ourselves and face the very sin that separates us from His love. It's time we became "The Church".

If we, as Believers, just sit still and listen for God's cry... What will we hear from Him? Are we ready to take up our cross and follow Him?

> *Mark 8:34 "Whoever desires to come after Me, let him*
> *deny himself, and take up his cross, and follow Me."*

Our Father doesn't want lukewarm followers. Listen to what Jesus said to the Lukewarm Church of Laodiceans in the book of Revelation:

> *Revelation 3:16 "So then, because you are lukewarm,*
> *and neither cold nor hot, I will vomit you out of My*
> *mouth."*

He is looking for men and women of valor. If we're honest with ourselves, truly honest, then we let Him prune out the deceptive lie of assumptions that poison the very foundation of our being!

Let God prune out the bitterness, the un-forgiveness, the hatred. May we move and shake up the world - leading the harvest of lost souls into the arms of the One Who is in love with His people.

Nothing, no nothing, is more important than living for God! Life makes no sense if we are groping around in the dark, stumbling over ourselves in ignorance and deceit.

> *Acts 17:27 "so that they should seek the Lord, in the*
> *hope that they might grope for Him and find Him, though*
> *He is not far from each one of us."*

The only real living you'll ever experience is being in His purpose, in the center of Life itself. No other place will satisfy your hunger for righteousness. All else will pale, all else will fail. Because, living for our Father God is the life He created us for. He is in love with His people. And a Father doesn't create us to be out of His plan or out of His will for our lives.

Believer, arise! Listen for the time draws near... The call to Believers, is a call to "Get Up"! Arise! Be awake. Be ready. Be on guard. The voice of the Master is calling us today....

"BELIEVER, ARISE!!"

> *1 Corinthians 4:8-9 "We are hard-pressed on every side, yet not crushed; we are perplexed, but not in despair; persecuted but not forsaken; struck down, but not destroyed."*

Notes and Reflections:

Notes and Reflections:

Chapter 7

"From Isolation to Inspiration"

I am the kind of person, that with much excitement I love to hear the voice of God guide me in every day actions or in trials of life. I am inspired by the Holy Spirit. I am waiting in anticipation to hear from Him to get my marching orders.

But I also am one to give up easily and call me and myself to a "pity party". Woe is little 'O Me!! Isolating myself when I'm struggling is the easy way out. If I can just get away from the world, even from my fellow sisters and brothers in Christ, I won't have to face my thoughts of failures.

And for the weak Believers, this is a well known place... It is a valley of isolation. It's during isolation that assumptions grow into all-out warfare in our minds. A battle that only grows larger with our aloneness.

I can remember being in a crowd of people and yet feeling like I was all alone in my depression. Feeling as if I was the only one who had ever thought bad things about others. Then as I grew in my walk with God, I realized there were others who struggled the same as I did! This is the very reason the enemy tries to keep us from joining other Believers. If he can convince us that we don't need others, we will never understand one another's battles or how they are the same battles as millions of other Believers.

If we become isolated and assume other Believers don't care... The enemy has deceived us into one of the greatest lies of all time. Because he knows we are stronger in numbers.

> *Ecclesiastes 4:9-10 "Two are better than one, because they have a good reward for their labor. For if they fall, one will lift up his companion. But woe is him who is alone when he falls, for he has no one to help him up."*

We've always heard... Two heads are better than one!! There is strength in sharing our struggles with one another.

Isolation is the breeding ground for assumptions. I had to isolate myself to think about suicide. I had to isolate myself to think about depression. But, once I shared it with my husband, the bondage was broken. No longer could it hold me in its dark grip of evil.

> *John 8:32 "And you shall know the truth, and the truth shall make you free."*

If we are to be inspired by the Holy Spirit, must die to ourselves. We must be set apart from the old man we use to be. We must put our best efforts towards living as He has called us to live. To do God's will no matter the cost. To become the Army of our God.

One way that we can grow in Him, is to read His Word and put it to action in our lives. I think of Ephesians 6 "The Armor of God". Because it's a spiritual war folks, we have to arm ourselves with His armor. I don't want to go to a fight ill-equipped!! I want to come out smelling like roses, not a burnt up pile of brush.

If you've become so comfortable in your isolation, that it's a chore even thinking about getting out of this rut... God wants to inspire you and wants you to win this battle. Don't assume the Church is against you, find out how others have struggled too. We are conquerors, together in this fight!! God designed us to win together, not separated from each other.

Notes and Reflections:

Notes and Reflections:

Chapter 8

"The Believer On Our Knees"

Prayer. So vital. And yet, so little used in our churches.

I am an intercessor. I say this like I'm at an AA meeting. "Hi, my name is Jennifer, I'm an intercessor." Because, sometimes interceding is one of the toughest jobs around!! It's hard to get past judgment of people and intercede for them. I mean, don't they realize they are making a mistake?? Don't they realize why they are in this mess??

I often ask God to remind me that without Him I am nothing. That I am just His vessel. God gave His Son to die for me... and how dare I whine and complain??

As Believers, we are called to pray, by getting on our knees and talking to our God. Change only comes through prayer. We want change, but we don't want to pay the price of taking time out of our hectic lives by spending vital time in prayer.

Selfish. Comfortable. Stubborn.

My cry to God right now is that He awaken all of us out of our stupor. That our minds are renewed for prayer. That our spirit man is awakened through His Word...

2 Chronicles 7:14 "If My people who are called by My name will humble themselves, and pray and seek My face, and turn from their wicked ways, then I will hear from heaven, and will forgive their sin and heal their land."

God is speaking to His Church, to Believers, to Christians, to you and to me.

We must seek God's face in prayer, because the very life of the world hangs upon our humility before Him. My heart cries out in intercession to God to heal my land!! To bring the lost to Him. For His people to awaken to this call upon the Believer.

If My people... He is speaking directly to you and directly to me. God's desire is for you and me to make a difference here on this earth.

It's pretty sobering to think the God of this universe wants US to pray. But this passage of scripture is very clear in its direction. Pray we must! Prayer will lead the way to revival in our land. I see a need for healing everywhere I look. How we must break God's heart. We know, we hear all about our world... the radio, television... but yet we chose to sit on our hands and not move from our comfort zone.

Prayer. None of us are exempt from the orders of prayer from our Father God.

God, I pray over the person reading this book that a new fire of prayer be placed in their heart! That they aren't content being passive in prayer. May they desire to hear Your voice in a much greater depth than ever before. I pray they cry out to You for change in our world. That they know from this moment on they are an intercessor. May they have an intimate relationship with You, to obey Your call on their life. May we be the Believer You've called us to be, and nothing less! May we have tenacity in our prayers and faith to see mountains moved in Your power. May we humble ourselves under Your mighty arm of righteousness and strive to live as You created us to live. May we have a heart as David, a heart that runs after You God. Use us to change this land. Heal our land we pray. Amen

Notes and Reflections:

Notes and Reflections:

Chapter 9

———— ⊗⊗⊗ ————

"Carrying Guilt"

I think each one of us at some point in our life has carried guilt of our past. Past mistakes we've made and had to deal with the consequences. And assuming then comes into play, crowding out balanced thinking.

Guilt seems to make a home in our mind without permission. It stakes claim where it's not wanted. Kind of like the weeds in our flower gardens, unwanted. Then it grows and causes chaos, where there use to be peace. Sound familiar?

Before we continue, I want to look at the meaning of guilt and decipher how God's Word heals this ploy of the devil.

Guilt = The feeling of responsibility or remorse for some offense, wrong, etc., whether real or imagined.

Here, I want us to recognize our Savior and how He took all of our infirmities upon Himself. It's not our responsibility to carry guilt!

If we could, we would go back and erase the wrongs we've done, right? I know I would if possible! But, we can't. So we have to let God's Word wash us and cleanse us of all wrongs. Begin each day new. God's mercies are new every day. And I want to live in His mercies every day, a fresh start.

It's very interesting to me how the end of the meaning of guilt was explained... real or imagined. Because, assuming is most of the time imagined in our mind. We play it again and again, over and over, in our mind how we should have done this, or how we should have said that.

While our actions can't be changed from yesterday... our thoughts can be changed by His Word today.

> *Hebrews 4:12 "For the word of God is living and powerful, and sharper than any two-edged sword, piercing even to the division of soul and spirit, and of joints and marrow, and is a discerner of the thoughts and intents of the heart."*

> *1 Corinthians 2:16 "For "who has known the mind of the Lord that he may instruct Him?" But we have the mind of Christ."*

Our enemy is just that... our enemy. He will take you out of the game of righteous living at all costs. Don't assume he's not seeking to devour you... He is. Carrying guilt is just one ploy he will load you down with.

Imagine the guilt Peter carried after he denied Christ, not just once, but three times! In one day! But, if you read the story further... Peter becomes a powerful preacher of God's Word and a man that even being in his shadow healed people. There are many more men and women of the Word that we could look at who had to deal with guilt. Like David's great story of killing a giant... and then he arranged for a man to be murdered in combat just so he could have his wife. Like Jonah, he ran from God's very evident call to evangelize Ninevah.

We all have a chance to carry guilt at some point in our lives. But our choice has to be to listen to God's words and let His love cover over our guilt. The scripture I think about here, is from Romans 8:1

*"There is therefore now no condemnation to those who
are in Christ Jesus"*

Guilt will come with condemnation. But God's love comes with no condemnation. People will judge with harsh condemnation. But God will love with an never-ending love. We have to recognize Who we live for. It's all about Him, living for God, and not for people.

True freedom comes through our choices. Make choices today that lead to truth and peace. Don't try to change what's already been done. Our past is our past. Keep it there. True healing comes in our future.

> *Dear Father God, help us to keep our minds on the truth of Your Word and to keep our past where it belongs, in the past. Help us to recognize the ploys of the enemy and to combat them with Your Word of truth. Truth always exposes the lies of the enemy. Thank You for sending Your Son to die for our sin. Help us to recognize who we are because of what You did for us. Help us to make choices based upon Your Word of truth. Thank You for Your Holy Spirit to comfort and guide us in our every day decisions. We have the mind of Christ. We will make decisions based upon the mind of Christ and the direction we get from You. Thank You for loving us just as we are! Amen*

Notes and Reflections:

Notes and Reflections:

Chapter 10

"Warfare with Worship"

Warfare = Conflict, especially when vicious and unrelenting, between competitors

Worship = Reverent honor paid to God; adoring reverence or regard

So, in this conflict, in this world... we are to worship God with unrelenting and vicious honor, adoring Him with reverence. That's a recipe for victory!!

If we look in the book of Psalms, we find so many scriptures that did just that... worshiped God!! With singing, instruments, laughter, shouting... God is calling us to worship Him in our everyday lives. With our every day jobs, every day families, every day words, every day prayers, every day of every day. With all of our being and all of our hearts lifted up to our Savior in adoration.

*Psalm 66:4 "All the earth shall worship You and sing
praises to You; they shall sing praises to Your name."*

It seems so easy when we read the Psalms, but on a bad day it's pretty hard to praise Him when there is a glitch in our life. It's not as easy said, as done.

I think we have to remember Who He is and not who we are. We have to fight with the Spirit and not with our flesh. Ephesians 6 gives us our armor. So, why aren't we putting it on? Why do we go day in and day out feeling defeated and alone? Why are so many Christians giving up on living for Him?

Here's the answer... It's war!! It's not an easy war either. If we are living for God with our all, then we will have to fight with our all. There is no other explanation. Look at the story of Elijah, he killed several men and then in the next chapter, he is running for his life. He was tired and felt defeated. But God came to him in the fire, in the wind, then in a small still voice. The God of Elijah's day is still the same God... He will reach you right where you are.

Remember, God reaches our brokenness with His love. He has done it over and over not only in our life, but in every life on earth. He loves you and He loves the world. He gave His Son for the world. He will speak in a still small voice to get your attention and get you back on track. He will speak to you through His Word and other times in a dream. Or maybe in a vision. Through prophecy. Through other people. He will get your attention.

He is speaking to you right now. I believe that if you are reading this book, God is speaking to you. You are meant to read what God has given to you. He wants you to know, there is no condemnation in Him. You are free from your past. You are no longer the man or woman you once were.

God has sent His Son to free you of bondages. But, freedom usually comes at a price. That price is giving your all to Him. Giving Him your life. Giving Him you and all that comes along with you. He knows everything about you and isn't surprised. He still loves you!!

Let His freedom wash over you and set you free. With worship doing warfare for your freedom. Worship and adore the One Who gave His all. With worship of our God and Savior comes freedom. And who doesn't want freedom??

Oh, heavenly Papa! Give us freedom to combat our assumptions. Give us Your mind, to wash over our guilt of the past. To cleanse our minds of all unrighteous thinking. Help us to concentrate on You and not on the past mistakes we've made. May we be changed and on fire to tell others about our freedom and about Your love for them. May we get over ourselves to love others! Help us to live a life that adores You so much, that we bring others into Your love and mercy. Thank You for Your mercies, new every day. May Your mercy shine so that others can see Your face in mine. Thank You for true freedom from the past. True forgiveness is mine and I'm thankful to You, my Savior. Amen

Notes and Reflections:

Notes and Reflections:

Chapter 11

"When Fear Grips"

2 Timothy 1:7 "For God has not given us a spirit of
fear, but of power and of love and of a sound mind."

I have struggled with a spirit of fear most of my life. Assumptions... fear
of death. Fear of the unknown. Fear of something that never happens. Fear
will strangle the life and faith completely out of your heart, soul and mind.

If God says He hasn't given us a spirit of fear, then where does fear
come from? It's pretty logical to recognize here that fear is from our enemy.
If fear grips you and you can't step out in faith, then the enemy has you
bound up in fear.

Psalm 34:9 "Oh, fear the Lord, you His saints! There is
no want to those who fear Him."

We have to realize that we are to "fear" God, in reverence and in awe.
This is a holy fear of the God of the universe. Of the God Who made the
heavens and the earth. Kind of like respecting those in authority over you.
Parents, bosses, government, etc.

As children of God, we are to respect our heavenly Father with a holy fear. I think of Moses up on the mountain called Horeb talking to God and how He had to keep His back to God, while God walked by. That is holy fear.

But for now, I want to talk about the fleshly fear. The kind that our enemy will try and stop us with. Fear of failure. Fear of rejection. Fear of loneliness. Fear of the unknown future.

As in the scripture in 2 Timothy... Love and a sound mind. A sound, balanced mind is by far the best weapon against our enemy. If we have it "together" in our mind, then our life will portray balance. But, if we are out of balance, out of order, more than likely most everything we do will be out of balance and have no order.

How do we get our mind balanced and in order? How do we "think" right?? It's in God's Word we find the peace and comfort for the unanswered questions of life. If we meditate on His Word, then our life will look like His Word.

2 Timothy 3:16-17 "All Scripture is given by inspiration of God, and is profitable for doctrine, for reproof, for correction, for instruction in righteousness, that the man of God may be complete, thoroughly equipped for every good work."

God gives us His Word to equip us in everything we do. Even against fear of lives failures. If you breathe, you will face failures. But the same breath has the Spirit of God living in it and is more than a conqueror!

Have you ever met someone who lives bound by a fearful life? Who couldn't ever get past their fear to live for God? If you are like me, you know way too many Believers who have allowed fear to grip their every move. I believe it's time to break free of the bondage of fear and to live as the Church, as God intended us to live... with victory to face the path we are on.

> *Romans 8:37 "Yet in all these things we are more than conquerors through Him who loved us."*

If we really believe God's Word is true, then we have the ability to conqueror our fears!! We are equipped through His Word to live in balance and in order. Because, if we, the Believer, do not live in balance, then we will never bring the lost to eternal life. Because we will be fighting just to get balanced and never able to help others see His hope.

It's very urgent for the Believer to be right where God intends us to be. It's through our love we will draw the lost into His embrace of eternal love. But if we can't find balance and order in our own lives, why would the rest of mankind desire a life like ours?

This is very concerning. The Believer has to rise up and become the Church of God Almighty to fulfill our commission to GO to the world. This makes me think and ponder my own life and how much I've not accomplished yet that God has called me to do. He has called us to GO...

> *Matthew 28:19 "Go therefore, and make disciples of all the nations, baptizing them in the name of the Father and the Son and of the Holy Spirit."*

We, Believers, must wake up and get this right!! We must be in balance to bring balance to the world. We must be in order and in agreement with one another. We have to listen for His voice and obey Him. He IS calling you to GO! Have you obeyed His voice and command? If not, today is never too late. He is an enduring God who loves us, even in our unbalanced state! He will call upon us right in the middle of our weakness. Because, when we are weak, He remains strong.

> *"My grace is sufficient for you, for My strength is made*
> *perfect in weakness."*

> *2 Corinthians, 12:9*

Maybe you've heard this spill before... Believer, arise to your commission and GO... But have we fulfilled this commission from God? Not yet! Otherwise, we'd all be in heaven with Him. So, this tells me, we still have a job to do here on this earth.

It is very important to remember, God's Word equips us. His Word will give us direction and correction. Meditate on His Word, walk as He has directed you to walk and draw in the lost.

> *Father, show us where our sphere of influence is and*
> *give us the wisdom to know when to GO and to know how*
> *to get there. Equip us with Your Word of truth and may*
> *we walk worthy of Your call upon our life. May we be Your*
> *hands, Your feet and Your mouth here on this earth. Give us*
> *a boldness to tell the world about Your love and hope. Give*
> *us a fire of excitement to light up this world with Your love.*
> *Thank You for Your Word that directs us and comforts us.*
> *Teach us to be just how You created us. May we know Your*
> *path for our life and walk as You give direction. Thank You*
> *for Your mercy and Your grace. Amen*

Notes and Reflections:

Notes and Reflections:

Chapter 12

"The Spiritual War"

2 Corinthians 10:3-6 "For though we walk in the flesh, we do not war according to the flesh. For the weapons of our warfare are not carnal but mighty in God for pulling down strongholds, casting down arguments and every high thing that exalts itself against the knowledge of God, bringing every thought into captivity to the obedience of Christ, and being ready to punish all disobedience when your obedience is fulfilled."

As I woke early this morning, my very first thoughts were on the past mistakes I'd made recently. "what if, should've, could've" But as I began to really wake up, I realized it was a deception from the enemy to get me off track, to start my day with him instead with my Savior and my God. And as I began to "change" my thinking, the Holy Spirit brought to my mind the above scripture.

This is a fighting scripture... a scripture full of war words and hope for every day.

So many days I begin with "what ifs, should've and could've" thoughts!! I want to take captive of these thoughts, I want to begin my day full of faith and full of fight. But, why don't I?? What is holding me back??

I pondered on Abraham, and how he must've felt climbing up Mt Moriah, taking his son to be sacrificed. Did he walk up that mountain thinking "my son is fixing to die" or did he think "no, my son will live"?? If we read the story and really study the walk of faith he was walking... we see he was trusting in God to free his son. He was walking in thoughts of "I believe in my God" and "If God says it, that settles it!" Abraham was being obedient against all odds. He was walking in a war most of us will never face. But what does God expect us to walk in today? Thoughts of the mistakes of the past, or in His walk of abounding faith??

So, I woke up assuming the worst before the day even begins!! I thought on this before even getting out of bed, before eating my breakfast, before my head was even clear!! First thing!!

This tells me if we are grounded in God's Word, we will fight the fight of assumptions and we will win with His Word. Even though I thought of the mistakes I'd made, the Holy Spirit brought His Word to my mind.

So, then, I knew there was hope for the day... direction in which way to go.

I can, I will, I am... with God's Word. But our flesh will remind us of "you should've, you aren't and you can't". Therefore, we must go to God's Word to figure out our "can-dos and what we already-haves".

I mean, if this is a war, then I want to win it, not lose. I want to be as Abraham and walk up my mountains knowing God will show up on my behalf!! But sometimes it feels like I'm trekking up a mountain with a 1,000 pound backpack strapped to my back!! I feel like I can't go on and why would I want to?

Defeat is not an option for us (Believers). This war is real, but we have God on our side. And if I can do all things with His strength, then this mountain is just another rut in the road.

> *Philippians 4:13 "I can do all things through Christ*
> *who strengthens me."*

So, hours later, another chapter later, I have hope renewed for another day. To fight with God's Word and not my fleshly mind. To fight as He equipped me to... with faith and my sword, which is the Word of God.

This day may prove to be a struggle, it sure started out that way. But with God's Word I will climb my mountain one more time and defeat the foe of assumptions that tries to deceive me into believing the lie. I will bring every thought into captivity and remind myself... you have the mind of Christ!

I urge you to read your Word and meditate on what God is telling you. Meditate on the words of the Creator of the universe. He wants you to walk in victory over the enemy. He wants you to take His hand and go up any mountain believing before you even begin "I can and I will". Be a little Abraham. Be what God has created you to be. If we are made in His image, then we are full of faith and love and every good work for His glory.

> *Jesus, our Lord and our Savior, cover our minds this day with Your love and Your wisdom. May our minds be captivated by Your Word and walk in faith as Abraham. May we walk in the Spirit and not the flesh, so we can prove to the world that You are God. Help us to begin each day with Your Word of encouragement and edification. Help us to believe if You said it, that settles it!! May our lives explode with Your faith and cause us to boldly proclaim Your love and Your goodness. Thank You Father for Your mercy, new every day. Amen*

Notes and Reflections:

Notes and Reflections:

Chapter 13

"Fainthearted Love"

John 15:12 "This is My commandment, that you love one another as I loved you."

When the Holy Spirit told me I was to write a chapter on love, I was so excited! But as I begin writing and thinking about love... how it must sadden God's heart how we don't love as He has called us to.

If we call ourself a Christian Believer, then we must be Christ-like, right? So, Christ was a friend with the sinners and tax collectors. He was right in the middle of the ones we sometimes try to get away from. Am I not speaking the truth here??

I think about the homeless or even the person who has no hope. I think about the person who walks into our pretty churches and were not accepted because of their clothes or their smell. I'm thinking about the person that hurt you really bad. Or maybe the person who spent the night in jail. Or the person who may have visited the local bar the night before.

We are called to love, no conditions attached. But so much of the time we, Christian Believers, attach all kinds of conditions to our love. But God loves unconditionally. And that's the kind of love He calls each of us to.

So are we fainthearted when it comes to loving people who are unlovable? Here I want to look at the word faintheart. And look at how God wants us to love.

Faintheart: Person who lacks courage; coward

Do we lack the courage to love as God loves? Are we all cowards when it comes to really loving? To really stepping out in His love? This would make sense to me. Because there are times I know I'm suppose to love, but yet I choose not to love. So much of the time, we assume God's people are either ok or that someone else will love them for us, so we don't have to.

You don't know how many times I've passed by the opportunity to love God's people and missed out on my blessing that God intended to give me.

But, I want to be a person who loves as God says to love...

> *1 John 3:16 "By this we know love, because He laid down His life for us. And we also ought to lay down our lives for our brethren."*

So, God, how can we lay our lives down for our sisters and our brothers? (It's not just our sisters and our brothers in the church either!!) We are called to love this forsaken world too!! So, how can I love as You command me to?? How can I love a person who is so hateful or who is just not easy to love??

I want to tell a story of love that happened to me. We had just started our business. I was helping a lot. Going to pick up parts and calling on people. I had to pick up parts at a certain office. The first time I called the office manager was so rude to me!! How dare she!! I got off and told Kevin, "Man was she rude!" Well after several months, of this person being rude

63

(and I was talking to her quite often)... the Lord told me "I want you to love her" I asked God.. "Oh my gosh Lord, how?" Because, I was assuming by her actions that she hated me for some reason.

Well I began to just take the time to ask how she was, and she began to open up to me a little at a time. She began to tell me the things that had happened in her life and I slowly was realizing why she was hurtful the way she was. She had so much pain and sadness happen in her life.

God wanted me to take the time to get to know her and to recognize her hurt. Hurting people really do hurt others.

As time went by, she became a friend and a person I love to talk to now. She calls me honey and hugs me so tight when I see her. I could see God's hand change that situation, all because I took the time to love. Seems simple, but it was a struggle to love as He wanted me to.

But we don't have a choice really, God commands us to love. He doesn't ask us to love. He commands us to!! There is a difference.

If God commands us to love, then He will equip us! I never thought I would be able to be friends with this person, I never thought God would use me the way He did. But He will, and He does.

I think of how Jesus must have been so hurt by Judas' betrayal. He knew Judas was going to betray Him way before it even happened. But He loved Judas anyway. This makes me think about how I've been betrayed, and how I reacted. Did I react in love or in hate? Most of the time, it was not love.

Love is a choice for you and for me. But it is a command from God.

1 John 4:8 & 11 "He who does not love does not know
God, for God is love. Beloved, if God so loved us, we also
ought to love one another."

It's pretty cut and dry. Pretty much to the point. We have to love, God says so.

I will tell you the truth, I have to work at loving some people and then there are others who are pretty easy to love. Sound familiar? I just imagine we can all think of people God has called us to love that we are having a hard time doing it!!

But, I do know love cuts through the harsh things of life and softens the heart. I've been there. I've seen it happen. Love.

Love: a profoundly tender, passionate affection for another person

I want to be a Christian who really loves. I want to make a difference in someone's life. Don't you? Because, if love is the answer, then we've got God's love, the answer, for the world. Right? Let's choose today to love and to bring God's love to the hurting.

> *1 John 4:20-21 "If someone says "I love God," and hates his brother, he is a liar; for he who does not love his brother whom he has seen, how can he love God whom he has not seen? And this commandment we have from Him: that he who loves God MUST love his brother also."*

So, as we finish this chapter, I leave with you... YOU have a choice to love. What will be your choice today? Ask God to give you love, He will. Ask Him to equip you with His heart of love, He will. Ask Him to send people into your life to love, He will. Believe you me!! He will!!

Choice: the right, power, or opportunity to choose; carefully selected

Unconditional: not limited by conditions

Make the choice today to love unconditionally!!

Help us, heavenly Father, to love through Your eyes of compassion. To see the person who You see. To see the potential that You have created in them. Help us to step out and love even when we don't feel so lovable. Help us to walk a love walk here on this earth. May we be Your hands, Your feet and go to the hurting and the lost. Give us compassion as You had compassion on us. May we show love in our actions and in our words. May we take the time and go out of our way for Your people. Remind us daily that You created people in Your image, and You command us to love them. Give us clean hearts. Hearts of compassion like You. Thank You for loving the world. For giving Your Son. For a love that's never failing. Thank You for the ability to love as You love. Amen

Notes and Reflections:

Notes and Reflections:

Chapter 14

"Frozen Faith"

How can I God?? How can I have enough faith to do what You've asked me to do?

Sound familiar? Our faith is frozen up by so many obstacles in our lives. Let me just say fear is our worst obstacle to faith. Faith is a step on the waters of unknown territory. Unknown waters we've never experienced before.

First, let's look at faith through God's eyes.... the faith of our Father and Creator, our King of kings and Lord of lords. Let's explore the only Book that can teach us about faith and build our faith up. Look at Hebrews 11:1...

> *"Now faith is the substance of things hoped for, the evidence of things not seen."*

Or, maybe the scripture from Romans 10:17...

> *"So then faith comes by hearing, and hearing by the word of God."*

I think each one of us reading this can say we've experienced a time we had to just stand on our most holy faith, trusting in our God. Remember Noah, wow. How he had to trust and have faith in what God had called him to! Imagine having to build a boat, (one you could not hide by the way), and there was no rain in sight!! Or imagine hearing the people's jeers and their laughing. You would be talk of the town, or possibly the world! You would be on tv for sure. "Wild man builds wooden boat, claiming GOD has told him to... and he even is saying we are all going to die! Where'd this guy come from??" Get the picture?

How many of us have had to stand on faith while there are others doubting our sanity? I think we can safely say every one of us have experienced some sort of scorn from someone. Or maybe we have scorned someone ourselves... ouch! Whichever the experience is with you or I, there is a certainty that we need to walk in a faith that is just too foreign to Believers nowadays.

Here's just one of my faith-walk stories... My husband and I kept hearing God tell us to sell our home... for no apparent reason. I went to God in prayer... "God, why would You ask us to sell our home?" Not long after praying, we also had confirmation from a few people that, yes, they also heard from God... We were to put our home up for sale. So we obeyed, and we put our home up for sale on a 6 month lease. Standing on our teetering faith, wondering why God would ask us to do this... Not one person, in that 6 months, not a soul, came to look at our house!! Boy, you talk about a faith walk. When neighbors asked in our small town "Why do you have your house for sale?" And we would say... "God told us to put it up for sale." (surprised faces) they would ask... "Oh, well where are you going if you sale?" And our reply was... "We do not know." (again, we got surprised looks of dismay) Their reply was... "Oh, ok..." Even some of our family were wondering what in the world we were doing!!

I'm sure you're wondering... did you sell your house?? No. We did not. At the end of the 6 months we figured out God was looking for our obedience. He wanted us to trust in Him... At this time, we have a business we currently are running out of our house and we have a machine shop on our property also. God, with His divine wisdom, knew all along what was in store for our future.

God has our best interest in mind. God has our futures right in the palm of His hand. What better place could we be!!

Let's look at what freezes our faith...

I'll begin by telling you I've dealt with some form of fear for about all my life. It is a battle to stop your mind from going into places of fear. For instance, if you watch the evening news there is all kinds of fear being voiced. There are so many avenues of fear creeping in to our lives. And, thank You God, there are many avenues of scripture to combat the fear.

Fear is a faith freezer.

But I believe that we ourselves are our worst enemy. I mean, if I read my Word I can glean from His Word and build myself up on my most holy faith. If I would just stop for a bit and pray to my Father, before I make any decisions... maybe it would keep me from fearing the unknown.

The unknown, that's something to think about... or maybe I should just put my future in God's hands, not fret about where I'll go next in life, or where I'll get the money to pay for that house... The unknown can trip us up faster than anything. We tend to think we have the right to worry about our future... but God wants us to trust in Him with all we have and all we do... Proverbs 3:5-6

> *"Trust in the Lord with all your heart, and lean not*
> *on your own understanding; in all your ways acknowledge*
> *Him and He shall direct your paths."*

Pretty plainly put, God wants our all, not part of our faith in Him, but ALL our faith in Him... Not trying to understand with our minds but understanding with His mind, His Word. When we trust in Him completely, this is the place where we can let Him direct our life and not depend upon ourselves. I've actually lived in both areas... Not trusting in Him, thinking I had total control. (Laugh!) And then I've lived on the other side of that, trusting completely in Him. I teeter totter back and forth some, but I'm learning more and more each day to trust Him.

So, I pray not only for you, but for myself too, that we get the revelation of trusting in Him and walking by faith. Because it's only in this faith walk that He can show us His promises. If I don't have faith in Him I'll never do His will. It takes faith to do everything in this life as a believer. If I don't trust Him I will never witness to the unbeliever. Because, without faith I cannot please Him. Hebrews 11:6...

"But without faith it is impossible to please Him, for
he who comes to God must believe that He is a rewarder of
those who diligently seek Him."

So, I must have faith to please my Savior. That's putting it pretty plain and simple. I must trust in God and seek Him and His ways diligently. With tenacity I must follow after His plan for my life. If I don't search for God's plan for my life, no one else will get it for me. If I don't step out in faith and listen for the Holy Spirit to guide me, I will miss what God has for me.

In closing out this chapter I just want you to know I'm praying for you and for your faith to be built up every day, for you to have tenacity and a determination to find out what a faith-walk is all about. I firmly believe most of us are missing out on a true faith-walk with God.

But there is always a new day and always a second chance with our Savior and King. He gave His Son, that's what we can stand on and that's what we can have faith in for the rest of our earthly lives.

Today, I pray you listen for the Holy Spirit and as you hear His voice, that you will trust in Him and walk out what He's calling you to.

> *Father, our holy Savior, I pray for each person who is reading this to get a new revelation of faith in You. With each word they read that You place a seed of faith in their spirit. That with each minute they breathe that they feel Your presence in a new and deeper way. That You will build them up and place in them a newness of life and a burning desire to follow after Your exciting ways and Your plans for their life. May You be number one in our lives this day and every day we serve You with an excitement like never before. That Your Word become like a fire and a hammer in our mouths. That we can make a difference wherever You call us to. That we can change the course of not only our own lives, but those around us be affected by Your presence in us. May we serve You with a tenacity and an expectation of what You are fixing to do in our lives. We praise Your holy name and we trust in You Father. Amen*

Notes and Reflections:

Notes and Reflections:

Chapter 15

"Birds Fly In Circles"

Opening up my eyes this morning, I instantly thought about my life and where I am in this season. It's not a fun season, to say the least. Different church, family in different season also, our business struggling, questions flying up to God "What's up??"... But amongst this season, I know that God has my back. The Holy Spirit brought to my mind the scripture about how God takes care of even the birds...

> *Matthew 6:26-27 "Look at the birds of the air, for they neither sow nor reap nor gather into barns, yet your heavenly Father feeds them. Are you not of more value than they? Which of you by worrying can add one cubit to his stature?"*

Let's look at this same scripture in the Message Version...

> *"Look at the birds, free and unfettered, not tied down to a job description, careless in the care of God. And you count far more to Him than birds."*

So, even in the dark seasons, God is in control of our lives. I think it's essential to put His Word down in our spirit man and try our hardest to live as He directs us. It is easy to say, but not as easy to live. I mean, worrying comes so natural. Living for God, living exactly how He tells us to, now that's hard!!

I grab my coffee and I sit back to hear from the Holy Spirit on where He is taking us in this season... I think about the mountains and the valleys we've been in lately. It's a down-right attack from our enemy and we know this. But, we must live in this world, we must confront this world's ideas, we have to live among the mayhem of the world. But, we can live separate and set apart lives. We can depend upon our God to change our circumstances and begin to walk as He would have us walk. But, it's just like swimming upstream, against the current. Or like trying to walk in a storm with hail beating down upon your noggin. I guess you get the picture...

My cry out to God is that I don't assume the world has the answers. That I look to Him for direction, even if the world looks like it has a better way. "EASY" just isn't in our vocabulary in this season!!

Our struggle isn't against flesh and blood, but against principalities of the air... against a darkness that's ready to take us out at any cost. I think it's imperative to separate this, in good situations and in the bad situations too. By separate, I mean, to recognize the enemy of our souls, to know that our struggle isn't of the flesh. To know that our struggles and our battles are fought with God, in our prayer closets.

Ephesians 6:12 "For we do not wrestle against flesh and blood, but against principalities, against powers, against the rulers of the darkness of this age, against spiritual hosts of wickedness in the heavenly places."

I can't assume it's always going to be this way, that it's just life, or that I am always going to struggle... that's just not what God intends for His children. And I am His child!!

I've heard sermon after sermon lately about the children of Israel, how they circled the Mountain of Sinai, and I've come to the conclusion that I don't want to circle anymore!! I want to get on the path that's straight and the path that leads to green pastures. I thought a circle was good, but it leads right back to where you've been in the past. It leads you right into its destiny of going backwards, not forwards.

So, I asked myself, am I walking in a circle God ordained or a circle that I have created? Because, remember, even those birds He talked about in Matthew 6 fly in circles!! But, I've figured out most of the circles I've walked around in are my own doing. My own ambitions and off the path God had intended for my life.

Stupid circles!! I mean, why can't there be squares, at least there would be corners we could rest in!! These circles of life are wearing me thin!! Don't you think that's just how them Israelites reacted to it too?? Whine, Whine, Whine.

Circles get me dizzy and make me want to crawl up in my bed and never get out again!! It's these circles though that lead me out of the dark seasons. If I didn't walk the circles of life, I would never get to my destiny God has planned for me. If I never walked these circles, I'd still be in a bed of nowhere-ness. So, the circles have a purpose. I just don't want to make the effort, or work at it, to find the purpose when I'm in such a dark place.

But, I have to discipline my flesh, tell it to die and get up out of that place of nothing-ness.

Galatians 5:24-25 "And those who are Christ's have crucified the flesh with its passions and desires. If we live in the Spirit, let us also walk in the Spirit."

God can't use me in nothing-ness. He can't speak to me through my circle-of-a-bubble I put up to keep myself safe from harm. I am of no use to God in a bubble of "don't bother me now God".

But, if we are truthful to ourselves, (God already knows), then we will fight to get out of that circle of nowhere-to-go. We have to choose to fight, otherwise, we'd never quit walking in circles, never quit being too dizzy to realize where we are!! If we keep circling, we become circlers of habit. Have you ever just done something because it was a habit? And not because it was right... We are creatures of habit. We sit in the same chair at church, we park in the same parking space in the parking lot, we drink coffee out of our favorite cup, we answer the phone the same way every time...

But it doesn't have to be a "habit" to do what God requires us to do to get out of that circle of nowhere-ness. If that bird doesn't have to worry about his food, God provides for him - then - God will provide for us a way out of the circle of habitual-ness.

If we stay in this circle of nowhere-ness, then we will always be circling around in our dizzy states, looking for reasons why God has done this to us... When all along we got ourselves in this circle-of-a-mess.

Assumptions remind me of a circle, they just keep coming, every day... sometimes the same ones bombard our minds even. They circle around and around in our head until we begin to believe them. As we allow ourselves to think about the assumptions, we will have to deal with them over and over. It seems this circle never ends!! Help, God!!

But now, may I present to you... The Way Out...

First, **STOP.** Stop going in circles. You do have control over your thoughts and actions. You do have the capability to live as God has commanded you to. Stop.

Secondly, **ASK.** Ask God to help you make the necessary changes to get out of the circle you're in. If you ask, God will answer. Sometimes it is not the answer we are seeking, but, nevertheless, He will answer. Ask.

Thirdly, **DON'T ASSUME.** Don't assume that it's ok to be in this circle. It's not. God is calling each of us to live outside the circle of "myself". If we don't live for Him, we are living for ourselves. (Ouch) Don't Assume.

Fourthly, **TODAY.** Start now, today, this minute. Don't wait for things to get better, it may be in this particular storm that you have the answer from Him how to move toward His destiny. We do not get to our God-given destiny inside the circle. Today.

STOP. ASK. DON'T ASSUME. TODAY.

Just imagine the world if all of us Believers would get out of the circle, really move toward God's destiny for our lives... This world would look a bit different, huh? Get real with yourself and make the necessary changes to get out of the circle of nothing-ness. If we put nothing in, we get nothing out.

> *Father, my God and Savior, Help us to make the changes that are necessary to get out of the circle of nothing-ness. Help us to recognize the reasons we are in this circle. Help us to trust in You to get us out. We can just be messed up sometimes, God!! Help us to get straightened up Lord. Help us to walk the narrow path of resistance, to not conform to this world or assume it's ok to walk with the world. Help us to go against the grain, to fight with Your Word. To recognize we win, that we are more than conquerors through You. May we find our destiny, Your plan for our lives, and not circle around one more time!! And may we defeat the nothing-ness habit of assuming it's ok to be in this circle. May we be*

Believers who live just as You intended us to live, in harmony with each other, walking together to make a difference in this world. May we be a light in this darkness of despair. Help us to walk as You created us to walk, in victory. Amen

Notes and Reflections:

Notes and Reflections:

Chapter 16

"Anger on My Mind"

Have you ever just woke up and you begin arguing before you even get your head up off of your pillow?? (I seem to do this a lot!) Yeah, that's what I did this morning as I woke up. Arguing with an unseen person, assuming the worst before I could even get out of my bed!

Our battle isn't against flesh and blood, but against principalities, rulers of the darkness... It's so apparent what our battle is, but how to fight the unseen battle is a whole other story!! We can fight with our own flesh or we can fight with the Word of God and the Holy Spirit. I've actually done both. And, I'll probably do both again and again.

There are battles we face every day as Believers. If you don't believe this, you will fight with your flesh. But once we get this revelation, that's when we begin to win the battle of the unseen, with the Sprit.

And assuming is one of the open doors to fighting with our flesh. We assume we know why that person didn't hug us in church, or we assume Pastor doesn't like us because he didn't recognize us in his sermon... Then, when we entertain these thoughts and they grow in our minds, this is the unseen battle of the flesh.

But, as we mature in our walk with God's Word, depend upon It for everything and let It wash us and cleanse us from all unrighteousness, this is fighting with the Holy Spirit and with power. We will win every time. By win I don't mean it feels good, or that we will hoop and holler along the way... No, by win I mean in the spiritual realm we win. It still is unseen.

This is one of the hardest walks for a Believer, to let go and let God. To trust even though we do not see...

Hebrews 11:1 "Now faith is the substance of things
hoped for, the evidence of things not seen."

Our battles are against unseen foes, enemies of our souls. And faith is what sees us through all our battles. Faith in the unseen. We can't touch, smell or feel our spiritual battles, but they are very real all the same.

Take for instance, fear. You don't see fear, you don't smell fear, and you can't feel fear with your fingers. But, as we all know, fear is real. Or anger, we can't touch or smell it but we know it's real. This is just a few examples of things we fight but can't see.

As Believers it is essential to recognize our battles are not against our spouse, our friends or our church family. But against spiritual wickedness of the air, rulers of the darkness. We have to recognize WHO we fight and HOW to fight against this enemy of the unseen world.

We tend to want to "ignore" the fact that there are spirits that exist just to torment us. We tend to want to not think about it, thinking then they will go away. We tend to think if we don't "stir" them up, we won't have to fight them. That's another tactic of the devil, to keep us in a state of denial.

Have you ever just been rocking along in life, all is hunky dory... and WHAM! You are facing a battle in your mind, out of nowhere?? Yes, if you are breathing, you have experienced this!! I am here to tell you, it's a real battle of the unseen forces of darkness. And the enemy doesn't play fair.

So, if the enemy is out to stop us, we have to be prepared and ready to fight and to win. There are far too many Believers who are losing!! And anger is just one of the many aspects we get tripped up over. We are angry at ourselves, we are angry at our families, we are angry at the way life has dealt us a bad one, we are angry because it feels good to "blame" someone else for our problems. We are an angry, out-of-the-will-of-God group of Believers.

We spend more time being angry at the way things are in life than we do just releasing it all to God. Ouch!! Therefore, we become so caught up in ourselves, we get way off the road of God's plan.

Let's look at what God says about anger...

Ephesians 4:26-27 "Be angry and do not sin: do not let the sun go down on your wrath, nor give place to the devil."

(MSG) 27 - "Don't go to bed angry. Don't give the Devil that kind of foothold in your life."

I can't even count the many times I've went to bed angry... And, the doors I opened for the enemy to work in my mind through assumptions. Let's look at the end of this chapter...

Ephesians 4:31-32 "Let all bitterness, wrath, anger, clamor and evil speaking be put away from you, with all malice. And be kind to one another, tenderhearted, forgiving one another, even as God in Christ forgave you."

There's that word again "forgiveness". Man, how many times do I have to be faced with having to forgive, when it's the last thing I really want to do?? Jesus said "seven times seventy" we must forgive. So, the answer to having a mind that's full of kind and loving thoughts? Forgiveness. Just as

Christ forgave us, we are to forgive everyone else around us. But, I know, that's easier said than done!!

I mean, look at what some people have done to me, or what they said, or what they caused in my life... Do I still have to forgive? Yes and you better forgive them!! I've found out the hard way if you don't forgive, you don't move from that place of bitterness. It's an awful ugly dark hole to live in un-forgiveness.

Anger will come, it's our flesh we are dealing with. The time we don't have to deal with anger, we will be in our spiritual bodies in heaven. Until then, let's fight against the tricks of the enemy and let's get into God's Word and become strong against the sway of the enemy. Let's win this battle against unseen foes. Let's get equipped to battle with faith and forgiveness. I'm not content to set on the sidelines and watch others serve God with their lives. I want to be a part of the Army of God. And I hope since your reading this, you do too.

It's not a party, it's not even fun all the time, but it is what God has called every Believer to do... live for Him. There are ups and there are definitely downs, but He always supplies us with what we need to get through everything we face. We have to "look" for and search for His ways and His righteousness. We can't sit by and hope things magically work out, we will be disappointed. God intends for us to read His Word, apply it to our lives and use it to fight the doors that open by assuming thoughts.

I am one of those who has to fight every day, I can't let my guard down and expect for things to be alright, it's not. It's a fight to the end, to the death. It's not a pinky swear kind of agreement. Satan is against us for real. We have to be aware of this and we have to fight the good fight of faith. With God's Word.

God will equip us with all the necessary tools to win. I want to win and I want to be a victor, not a loser. God has given me this book for the benefit of myself and for Believers. The Holy Spirit is preparing us and teaching us along the way. That's my kind of army!! God as my Chief Commander, leading from the Holy Spirit and Jesus as my Savior along for the ride. Woo Hoo! Give me my saddle, put me aboard and let's get with this!!

This makes me think of a man who came to a church I was attending... He was talking about the enemy and our faith. He said he told the devil every day "How do you like me now Satan?!?" That's a victory call! That's what we all need to live by... Winning the battle against our enemy and defeating the assumptions that try to take us out of the frontlines of victory.

It behooves me to say... Always put on your armor... That's how we will end this chapter... Ephesians 6:10-13

"Finally, my brethren, be strong in the Lord and in the power of His might. Put on the whole armor of God, that you may be able to stand against the wiles of the devil. For we do not wrestle against flesh and blood, but against principalities, against powers, against the rulers of the darkness of this age, against spiritual hosts of wickedness in the heavenly places. Therefore take up the whole armor of God, that you may be able to withstand in the evil day, and having done all, to stand."

Notes and Reflections:

Notes and Reflections:

Chapter 17

———— ⊂∞∞⊃ ————

"This Journey"

In my Christian walk, I've had the privilege to go to several different countries on mission trips. I've been to Mexico, Romania, Africa and Brazil. But, I also know my mission field is right outside the front door of my home.

God has given me a sphere of influence wherever I go. An authority to walk this earth with strength and might from Him.

There are lots of different "shoes" we wear on this journey of life. This journey of being a Christian. This journey of struggles.

I think about the shoes of joy and laughter, or the shoes of weeping and sadness, and also the shoes of life or of death. There are many different avenues in life we travel. But there is only one way to travel with God, the shoes of holiness. We are to be set apart, to be different, even odd to the world. But so much of the time, we try to fit-in to the standards of the world, instead of being separate from it.

> *"but as He who called you is holy, you also be holy in*
> *all your conduct."*
> *1 Peter 1:15*

In all of my assuming and thoughts, it has brought me to times in my life when I cared more about what people thought than about what God wanted. I assumed people wouldn't like me if I didn't say or do the things they expected of me. This is another area we have to re-teach our minds, work at conforming to God's Word, and not to the world view of ourselves.

We are so much like the children of Israel, roaming around and having to go around that mountain so many times!! Not learning our lesson the first time… You know some of them were saying "God, help us to learn this so we don't have to repeat it again!!"

How many times have you told God just that? If you are like me, numerous times. I've ran around the same life mountain again and again. When will I learn??

But, God, in his infinite mercy, keeps holding my hand… patiently telling me (AGAIN) how to walk this journey.

In this journey, I want to find my promised land of milk and honey. I don't want to continue to go around and around. And I do think it is possible to learn the first time.

Here again, we must know God's Word and His promises to get it right the first time!! Look at this scripture in Jeremiah 29:11

> *"For I know the thoughts that I think of you, says the*
> *Lord, thoughts of peace and not of evil, to give you a future*
> *and a hope."*

God wants a future for us, and a hope, good things for His children. So, how do we mess it up so much of the time? Glad you asked…

Because, God has given man choice. We are the ones who have messed up our own lives. God wants good and a future for us. Hope for us. We, in this process, make choices that detour our lives off His path for our future.

My testimony is very fitting for this... Kevin and I got out of church, starting running from God. Bars, drinking and all that went with that scene. We ran hard from the call on our lives. We ended up almost divorcing through this time. But, God had a future and He had a hope for our marriage!! We got our lives straight with Him and we choose our footsteps very wisely now. We have been married 36 years!! Our marriage is a miracle from God.

But, we made the choice to run and to do the things we did during this time of running from God's plan. We were the ones who did this. Not God.

Your choices today will affect your life in the future. Don't let the enemy tell you it's okay. Make the choice to walk as God has called you to walk. In holiness through Him.

Choices are so vital to our walk with God. We must choose to obey Him in all we do and in all we say. Romans 8:1 talks about our walk in the Spirit...

> *"There is therefore now no condemnation to those who*
> *are in Christ Jesus, who do not walk according to the flesh,*
> *but according to the Spirit."*

We have to walk as God calls us to walk... in the Spirit. In our journey, we will get there much faster if we are just walking with Him.

Have you ever walked down a sidewalk with someone and held their hand? This is a picture of walking with someone. Not against them. And this is the same way God expects for us to walk... with Him, not against Him. Living away from God's will is like swimming against a very strong current of waves.... I know, I ran from God's plan for about 6 years of my adult life. And it's hard when we fight against the very Creator of our souls.

The results of a walk without God are usually not too pretty. But, you know, even in the Israelites disobedience, God still sent a cloud by day to shade them and food every day to feed them. God still does this for us today. He is still the same God. He provides for His children.

So, in ending this book, I will implore you to choose His direction for your life. Choose His holiness to live by. Be separate from the world, be different. Go against the normal. God is calling us as Believers to conform to His ways, not the world's ways.

I want to end this book with the greatest way I can, in prayer. Remember, I am praying for you and for your life to look like Christ. Don't ever give in to the enemies tactics. Keep going in the direction God has called you to go. Don't give up. He is with you forever.

Hebrews 13:5 "Let your conduct be without covetousness; be content with such things as you have. For He Himself has said, "I will never leave you nor forsake you."

Father God, may we be Your people in everything we do and everything we say. Help us to conform to Your image and not the world's view of how we are to act. May we think Your Word and live Your Word in all we do!! Help us to listen to the Holy Spirit and walk as children of Your light. Give us a heart to be as You are, holy. For You have called us to be holy and to live separate from the world. We're not always a good example of Your Word, so help us to become an example people want to follow, which leads them to You and to Your love. Could You please show us the path we're to take in this world? Show us the love You have for others so we can bring them to the Cross and to Your salvation. We love You Father God, we are Yours. Please use us to change those You have given to us to witness to. May we love as You command, unconditionally. Help us to remember the Cross every day that we see Your people. Because, without the Cross, we wouldn't be living. With You, life is all worth it. We give You the praise and the glory our Lord! Amen!!

Notes and Reflections:

Notes and Reflections: